The media's watching Vault!
Here's a sampling of our coverage.

"For those hoping to climb the ladder of success, [Vault's] insights are priceless."
– *Money magazine*

"The best place on the web to prepare for a job search."
– *Fortune*

"[Vault guides] make for excellent starting points for job hunters and should be purchased by academic libraries for their career sections [and] university career centers."
– *Library Journal*

"The granddaddy of worker sites."
– *U.S. News and World Report*

"A killer app."
– *The New York Times*

One of Forbes' 33 "Favorite Sites"
– *Forbes*

"To get the unvarnished scoop, check out Vault."
– *Smart Money Magazine*

"Vault has a wealth of information about major employers and job-searching strategies as well as comments from workers about their experiences at specific companies."
– *The Washington Post*

"A key reference for those who want to know what it takes to get hired by a law firm and what to expect once they get there."
– *New York Law Journal*

"Vault [provides] the skinny on working conditions at all kinds of companies from current and former employees."
– *USA Today*

VAULT
> the most trusted name in career information™

VAULT CAREER GUIDE TO
PHYSICAL THERAPY

VAULT CAREER GUIDE TO
PHYSICAL THERAPY

DR. ANNLEE BURCH
AND THE STAFF OF VAULT

Library of Congress CIP Data is available.

ISBN 13: 978-1-58131-449-6

ISBN 10: 1-58131-449-3

Printed in the United States of America

ACKNOWLEDGMENTS

Annlee Birch's acknowledgments: Thanks to my husband Steve.

Vault's acknowledgments: We are extremely grateful to Vault's entire staff for all their help in the editorial, production and marketing processes. Vault also would like to acknowledge the support of our investors, clients, employees, family and friends. Thank you!

Wondering what it's like to work at a specific employer?

Table of Contents

Visit Vault at **www.vault.com** for insider company profiles, expert advice, career message boards, expert resume reviews, the Vault Job Board and more.

VAULT CAREER LIBRARY

ix

Introduction

Physical therapy is a growing profession with four areas of practice: examination of individuals with impairment, functional limitation and disability; treatment of impairment and functional limitation through therapeutic intervention, which includes exercise, patient education and application of modalities; consultation; and research. Physical therapists evaluate ill or injured persons to determine what functional limitations are present. For example, a young man who suffers from spinal cord injury will have strength and flexibility limitations in various muscle groups depending on the level of injury. A young woman with multiple sclerosis may have functional limitations in balance and coordination.

Initial evaluations performed by the physical therapist include measurements on a wide battery of abilities. Physical therapists measure an individual's capability in domains including strength, endurance, flexibility, coordination, balance, gait, skin integrity and ability to perform simple activities of daily living. After initial evaluation of a patient, the physical therapist will identify a set of problems with physical function and assess how these problems may best be approached through exercise, massage or a modality (treatment applications other than exercise, such as hot/cold packs, ultrasound—healing through deep sound technique—or electrical stimulation).

Physical therapists today also act as consultants through their knowledge of exercise, and those in clinical and academic settings are also involved in research projects to determine whether the treatment interventions they are currently using are grounded in theory and to determine how best to improve upon interventions. In today's health care arena, physical therapists must be patient advocates—that is, balance the dual roles of providing expert information to patients on all types of disease and injuries, allowing the patient to play an active role in choosing options for treatment.

Visit Vault at **www.vault.com** for insider company profiles, expert advice, career message boards, expert resume reviews, the Vault Job Board and more.

VAULT CAREER LIBRARY

1

Use the Internet's
MOST TARGETED
job search tools.

Vault Job Board

Target your search by industry, function and experience level, and find the job openings that you want.

VaultMatch Resume Database

Vault takes matchmaking to the next level: post your resume and customize your search by industry, function, experience and more. We'll match job listings with your interests and criteria and e-mail them directly to your inbox.

THE SCOOP

What Do Physical Therapists Do?

CHAPTER 1

Students of physical therapy are taught that their patients will not achieve maximum functional capabilities unless the physical therapist listens to the patient, advocates for the patient and stays current in all aspects of practice. It's a common public misperception that the doctor is the diagnostician and the physical therapist follows his directive for treatment. This is ancient history; nowadays PTs are expert evaluators and clinicians for all physical diagnoses. A medical doctor may refer a patient suffering from a cerebral vascular accident (CVA) or a stroke to a physical therapist, but it is the PT, then, who evaluates strength, range of motion, balance, gait and coordination and documents what variations from normal expectations are found.

In other words, PTs look at a whole battery of parameters to see whether or not the person has a functional limitation. Some evaluations are quantitative (using measurements that are numerical and objective) and some have a qualitative element (based on therapist's opinions and perceptions). Some involve manual measurement; others, measurement using technical equipment. The manual muscle test is an example of a manual battery used to measure a patient's strength. The physical therapist applies manual resistance to all muscle groups and grades the deficits on a scale of 0-5. The BIODEX is an example of a technological evaluation and treatment tool where muscles are evaluated for strength by a machine set to read force output. A critical evaluation tool is simply the ability to listen to the patient and her complaint.

Evaluation

Physical therapists evaluate patients for functional problems, designing treatment plans for patients with a specific outline of short- and long-term goals. Cases might include learning to walk again, increasing muscular strength of any weakened musculature, decreasing pain that is interrupting enjoyment of life, increasing range of motion of joints, improving balance and increasing coordination, and often these goals are achieved through the collective efforts of an interdisciplinary team (a team of different medical professionals), patient and family members.

When a physical therapist evaluates a patient (regardless of whether she is working in a direct access or non-direct access state), evaluation is divided into two parts. There is a subjective portion of the evaluation, in which the therapist listens to the patient's history and story of injury or illness, and there is an objective portion, where the therapist conducts a series of tests for strength, flexibility, balance, coordination, skin integrity and more. Physical therapists learn not only to be compassionate and attentive listeners but also to be acute observers of physical strengths and deficits. She is looking to connect a deficit in an area such as strength or balance with a "functional" deficit; in other words, a deficit on a quantitative test is connected to what portion of the patient's physical function and quality of life is being affected. Once limitations are found, the physical therapist writes down, or "documents," baseline measures and later compares these with how far the client progressed or improved with treatment.

Not all personnel in the field of physical therapy are licensed to evaluate and treat patients. The two professional rungs in the field of physical therapy are the physical therapist and the physical therapist assistant. A physical therapist assistant (PTA) is an individual who completes a two-year associate degree undergraduate program and is able to provide treatment only, under the direction of a physical therapist; a PTA is not licensed to evaluate patients. Nonprofessional personnel include physical therapy aides, who provide set-up, maintenance of treatment area and scheduling services.

Empirical evidence

Academics and clinicians in the field of physical therapy are focused on providing treatment guided by empirical evidence. Compared to the fields of psychology and medicine, for example, the emphasis on empirical evidence to justify treatment is more recent in physical therapy. Progressive resistive exercise (exercise using increasing amount of weight resistance with a specified number of repetitions) has been used to strengthen musculature for at least a century, and consistent systematic reviews of randomized clinical trials to determine whether progressive resistive exercise strengthens muscles more effectively than no exercise have only been conducted in physical therapy over the past 20 years. In today's health care environment, students and practicing physical therapists demand evidence supporting the proven effects of treatments they are using and that such treatments can be verified with published research. Students entering the field of physical therapy today will encounter colleagues who have published, taught, developed a clinical expertise niche or done a little of it all. The possibilities in the field are endless. Today the American Physical Therapy Association urges all practicing physical therapists to enroll in continuing education classes to keep skills up to date and with a scientific edge. Most professionals do so gladly and are often reimbursed by the sites/programs at which they work.

Physical therapy educational programs strive to provide students with as much about what it is like to have a disability, injury or illness as possible. PT students not only study the anatomy and physiology of the human body but also participate in discussions and courses centering around the psychosocial needs of persons with disabilities. PT programs include sections on the legal ramifications of being disabled and PTs in and out of school must stay up to date on all aspects of health care policy and how it affects their patients through continuing education, referred journals and the media.

Diagnosis

As physical therapy moves from requiring a master's degree to a clinical doctorate, physical therapists are performing not only evaluation, but functional physical diagnosis, as a doctor would. In the past, physical therapists were only expected to evaluate and treat patients, but the increasing number of clinical doctorates in the field is elevating those therapists' role in the treatment process.

Goals: long-term and short-term

To help individuals achieve maximum functional capabilities in order to continue to live as full a life as possible, physical therapists set short- and long-term goals at the time of evaluation for all patients. An example of a short-term goal for a patient with a low back injury may be to decrease the pain level from a level of 9/10 (extreme pain) to 7/10 (moderate-high level pain). An example of a long-term goal for a patient with low back injury may be to have the patient be able to return to work or school. Physical therapists are trained to write all goals as measurable items, primarily because insurance companies reimburse objective and quantifiable measures. It's important to look for places of employment that allow enough time for documentation of these goals and other note writing. Increasingly, due to managed care, the complexity of federal and nonfederal insurance rules and patient liability issues, there is more and more paperwork required by all professionals working with patients. Daily duties for the physical therapist involve not only evaluating and treating patients but also writing down all findings and treatment in measurable terms carefully and consistently. A good place of

Visit Vault at **www.vault.com** for insider company profiles, expert advice, career message boards, expert resume reviews, the Vault Job Board and more.

V/\ULT CAREER LIBRARY

7

employment allows the physical therapist enough time for note writing so that the copious paperwork stays under control and the therapist does not have to stay late after hours to keep up with it. Many places of employment now encourage PTs to input data into a computer, thus saving time for the therapist and standardizing note writing across the organization.

While typical diagnoses physical therapists evaluate and treat include orthopedic injuries such as bone fractures or muscle strains/sprains, neurological conditions such as stroke and spinal cord injury, cardiovascular conditions including asthma and heart conditions, physical therapists treat conditions that affect a myriad of systems in the body. And people often have more than one problem at a time, which is referred to as a dual diagnosis. Increasingly, patients are more knowledgeable about medical conditions largely because of Internet access, so physical therapists often evaluate patients who have researched their own condition. This means that the PT sometimes has to spend time reeducating the patient with accurate information about physical therapy procedures, so it's critical that the PT have a love of lifelong learning to stay abreast of all the changes in health care treatments.

Treatment

Physical therapy treatments, as defined by the APTA, include exercise, functional training, training in the use of assistive devices such as canes, walkers and crutches, manual techniques including massage, mobilization and manipulation, airway clearance techniques, which are used to clear blocked breathing passages in pulmonary therapy, and ultrasound, electrical stimulation and traction.

Exercise

Physical therapists must promote the power of exercise, both aerobic and anaerobic. Aerobic exercise (riding a bike for 15 minutes or more, vigorous walking for 30 minutes, running for 10 minutes, swimming) increases circulation to the heart, improves lung capacity and increases endurance for greater periods of exercise. An individual recovering from a heart attack or stroke with the proper precautions will benefit greatly from aerobic exercise as improved circulation, cardiovascular health and aerobic endurance has been proven to protect against future heart attacks or strokes. Aerobic exercise is beneficial to all ages and for many illnesses. (Currently there is an obesity epidemic among America's children and aerobic exercise is directly linked to a healthy weight in children.) Anaerobic exercise is exercise of shorter duration where the emphasis is on force output versus sustained activity. Examples of anaerobic exercise would be a bench press of less than three repetitions, jumping from a standing position in basketball, or a wrestler pinning an opponent down in less than three minutes. Anaerobic exercise challenges muscles to their ultimate force output and stretches fibers to increase muscle bulk. Physical therapists use anaerobic exercise to increase muscle strength in patients who are weakened through many different illnesses and injury.

Physical therapists "prescribe" exercise for infants, children, young and older adults, and those considered to be very old (85 and up). Public health experts today are calling on physical therapists for advice and consultation on all types of morbidity epidemics such as childhood obesity, cardiovascular disease and osteoporosis, so in many cases, physical therapists can augment clinical practice (clinical practice is defined as the evaluation and treatment of patients in need of physical therapy services) with private consultation to companies, nonprofit organizations or schools. Aside from knowing how much and what kind of exercise to prescribe, physical therapists should also know all contraindications (when NOT to prescribe) exercise.

Manual therapy

Physical therapists use their hands to work, called "manual therapy" in PT vernacular.

Manual therapy includes techniques for stretching, strengthening and reducing pain. Physical therapists may use massage as a manual technique for reduction of pain. Techniques include effleurage, a massage technique from Sweden in which broad strokes are used to increase circulation throughout the body; acupressure, which identifies trigger points through deep pressure; and friction massage, quick, brisk movements in the direction opposite fibers' alignment to interrupt neuronal pain signals and increase circulation. Depending on the type of injury, a therapist may choose effleurage to relax tense musculature throughout the body, trigger point massage to release a specific tight muscle (the trapezius, for example, is often tight due to poor posture), or friction massage for an injury like a sprained ankle, in which specific massage at the site of pain can complement rest, ice and elevation. Physical therapists also perform mobilization techniques, a method by which tissue is moved to reduce pain. There are four grades of mobilization (1-4) from most gentle to more forceful pressure. PTs also perform myofascial treatment (moving the fascia of the body to reduce pain) without instruments, only hands. Myofascial treatment has been proven to be very effective with chronic pain patients. Craniosacral therapy is another type of manual treatment in which the cranium (the skull) and the sacrum (the portion of the backbone between the coccyx and the low back) are mobilized and massaged to relieve pain. Craniosacral therapy is effective in reduction of migraine headaches, arthritic pain and many types of chronic pain.

All physical therapists have the ability to do manual therapy and are schooled in different techniques of massage and mobilization (moving soft tissue and bones manually). However, some physical therapists find career tracks that take them away from direct contact with the patient. Physical therapists who become teachers and administrators will be less adept at manual therapy techniques because of lack of daily practice than those who evaluate and treat patients for a living. Some physical therapists become famous because of the effectiveness of their manual skills. Ted Corbitt is a renowned manual therapist who gained a national reputation over more than 25 years at the International Center for the Disabled in New York. A long-distance runner, he also created the idea for the New York City marathon with Fred Lebow.

Modalities

When physical therapists are not treating patients with manual therapy or exercise they may be providing so-called "modality" treatments, which include use of whirlpools, paraffin treatments (hot wax), electrical stimulation or ultrasound (healing by sound waves). Whirlpool treatment may be used to clean wounds after injury, and also helps decrease swelling. Paraffin is often used for the hands and feet to relieve arthritis-related joint pain. Electrical stimulation is often used after a neurological injury, such as stroke, to stimulate nerve action potential and regain movement. Ultrasound is used to decrease pain and increase circulation after any injury, and the theory is that sound waves make this possible.

Physical therapists also provide their patients with advice about their physical problems, providing tips for reducing physical stress and strain, options for exercise once at home, as well as counsel on postural alignment, healthy work environments, even the right shoes.

Jobs in the Industry

Physical therapists are frequently employed in schools, hospitals (including acute care hospitals), rehabilitation centers, health clubs, nursing homes, community centers or in private practice. Because of the nature and diversity of the work, physical therapists have very flexible schedules and can work part time, full time or a combination of the two.

Physical therapists' working days are most often 50 percent routine and 50 percent innovation. Though the need to evaluate and offer a functional diagnosis remains constant, there is no assigned "template" for treatment. The physical therapist uses clinical evidence, past experience and problem-solving skills in the context of the patient's needs and his current condition before designing the best treatment plan.

Where do Physical Therapists Work?

Any health care facility, acute care hospital, health club, nursing home or outpatient center, depending on its own internal budget and staffing needs will at times require full-time help and at other times only part time. A physical therapist with young children may decide to work a three-day week and consult to augment earnings. A new physical therapist may decide to work long hours for the first three years and then taper off to part-time clinical work if teaching appeals to him. Physical therapists become highly organized persons by necessity, as they are often juggling patient caseloads, learning and applying new scientific information and pursuing specialty practices, so the variety of options tends not to be too overwhelming for most.

Much of the time, physical therapists evaluate and treat individuals who have suffered from a traumatic injury such as a head injury, spinal cord injury, bone fracture or have an acute or chronic disease such as Parkinson's, cancer, HIV/AIDS or multiple sclerosis. In addition, physical therapists may also be called upon by sectors of the community, such as government officials, teachers, scientists or other health care professionals for advice and expert knowledge about muscle injury and a broad range of chronic and acute disease.

There are so many different places to practice as a physical therapist, most PTs are able to find the patient population they are most interested in treating. From acute care to pediatrics, there is something for everyone.

Acute care hospitals

Acute care hospitals in both urban and rural settings hire physical therapists to work in a rotational mode: PTs may start in an orthopedic unit treating fractures, hip replacements and shoulder injuries, and move to a burn unit or a neurological unit. This way, hospitals are assured all areas are covered, and at the same time, the entry-level physical therapist is exposed to all sorts of patient groups.

The acute care setting is fast-paced and requires the physical therapist to work as a member of an interdisciplinary team that may include a social worker, doctor, nurse, occupational therapist and speech therapist. As a member of the acute care team, the physical therapist sees patients immediately after acute injury and illness, and often evaluates patients before and after surgery. For instance, an 85-year-old woman suffering from a fracture to the hip may require a total hip replacement. The therapist must evaluate this patient's strength, range of motion, balance and coordination after the injury, before surgery and after surgery. Exercise intervention would be cautious and determined by level of pain and flexibility limitations.

Schools

Elementary schools throughout the U.S. hire physical therapists on nine-month schedules to provide therapy to disabled students. Schools look to hire PTs who express a deep interest in pediatrics, and will hire both entry-level and experienced PTs. Many PTs enjoy working in schools because of the flexibility of scheduling and relative autonomy (without the hierarchy of a hospital) that the environment lends.

A physical therapist working in the school system sees the very young client versus the very old. In the United States, and some other parts of the world, children with disabilities are integrated into schools with the nondisabled. The disabled pediatric population needs the services of physical therapists, occupational therapists and often speech therapists. The physical therapist working in the public schools works a September to June schedule with summers off, and daily working hours often vary. School systems also require that a physical therapist work as a member of an interdisciplinary team (teacher, parent, student, physical therapist, occupational therapist and speech therapist), but the therapist will have more autonomy than the hierarchy of an acute care hospital allows.

Rehabilitation centers

Rehabilitation centers across the nation may specialize in head injury, cancer or spinal cord injury, or may serve more than one patient group; such centers employ physical therapists to lead a patient after injury through what is often a six-month course of rehabilitation. Nursing homes hire physical therapists to provide therapy to both the well elderly (to maintain physical function) and the ailing elderly (to improve physical function).

Rehabilitation centers focus on returning patients to a way of life that most resembles what life was like prior to injury. Physical therapists will often see patients every day or three times a week, and work over a period of three months or more to enable a spinal cord-injured patient to be able to move from a bed to a chair, or to enable a brain-injured patient to walk 200 feet without falling.

Fitness centers: health clubs and sports clinics

Sports clinics, which are facilities that treat sports injuries, hire physical therapists with one to two years of experience and want the PTs to have some manual skills under their belt and an express interest in sports physical therapy.

When a physical therapist works in a fitness center, his focus is on exercise, either as prevention to illness or as a way to maintain a healthy lifestyle. A physical therapist may also evaluate and treat minor sports injuries that occur as a result of excessive or ill-advised exercise. The fitness center therapist may work with persons with or without disabilities who wish to stay healthy through exercise.

Nursing homes

Nursing homes will hire both entry-level and experienced physical therapists interested in the aging adult. Nursing homes (SNFs) often carry the stigma of an unpleasant place to work but modern SNFs (skilled nursing facilities) differ from the nursing home of the 1970s and have a combined patient population of young and old.

A physical therapist working in a nursing home or SNF needs to be comfortable with and skilled at working with the old, severely disabled and terminally ill population. The major difference for the physical therapist working in the nursing home or SNF is that the patients he or she sees will not be discharged to home. They will stay at the respective facility their

Visit Vault at **www.vault.com** for insider company profiles, expert advice, career message boards, expert resume reviews, the Vault Job Board and more.

VAULT CAREER LIBRARY   13

whole lives, and this difference can take an emotional toll on the physical therapist as patients often suffer from depression.

Interdisciplinary Teams

Wherever he works, a physical therapist is a member of an interdisciplinary team. This generally includes the physician, social worker, occupational therapist, respiratory therapist, speech therapist, nurse, patient's family and the patient. Most of us are familiar with what doctors and nurses do, but what about the other allied health fields? Here's a brief description of what each of these professionals adds to the patient's care.

The occupational therapist offers skilled treatment to help individuals achieve independence in all facets of their lives. Services may include a comprehensive home and job site evaluation to determine what adaptive recommendations may be needed (an elevated stool to reach the counter in the kitchen, assistive equipment to open jars and bottles if the patient has weakened grip strength; auditory additions to a computer in the workplace if the person has compromised hearing, etc.).

Social workers carry out treatment, counseling and oversee other services to help solve immediate financial, housing and social problems for each patient and to determine whether the problem is an individual one or whether there is a larger system issue. For instance, a social worker would assist a patient having trouble understanding how to use her Medicare card. The social worker would then determine if there was a larger system issue at hand, such as if the directions were not written in Spanish, and the majority of community members spoke Spanish only.

The respiratory therapist's day includes all aspects of evaluating and treating breathing capacities in patients of many different diagnoses. The respiratory therapist must be able to clear breathing passageways with the appropriate technology, respond to emergency situations when patients lose breathing capacity due to environmental trauma (fire) or physical trauma (abuse), and be able to educate and train parents and patients dealing with respiratory weakness due to asthma or another problem.

The speech therapist evaluates a patient with speech disorders and develops a treatment plan to improve speech patterns and communication skills. Speech is commonly disrupted after stroke and head injury, but persons may also be born with speech deficits in diagnoses such as cerebral palsy. All members of the allied health care team keep one another informed of their evaluative findings and choices of treatment so that patients receive the best care possible.

Interdisciplinary teams are the norm in acute care settings, nursing homes and some comprehensive outpatient care units. In a home-care setting, the physical therapist works independently but will communicate with all other members of the interdisciplinary team on an ongoing basis. The sports physical therapist and the physical therapist in private practice will usually not work with other members of the health care team on site, but will communicate through verbal or written correspondence. At a hospital, the physical therapist is active in discharge planning for the patient, which is the health care team's strategy for transitioning the patient from a hospital to a long-term care facility or to a nursing home or other home with an informed social support system, adapted to the patient's injury or illness. Patients are always discharged from acute care hospitals (unless they die while in acute care). Discharge planning is central to the PT's role because the PT decides whether a patient is safe to walk, climb stairs, drive a car, go back to work or lift children.

Visit Vault at **www.vault.com** for insider company profiles, expert advice, career message boards, expert resume reviews, the Vault Job Board and more.

VAULT CAREER LIBRARY   15

Industry Trends

As the physical therapy industry grows, there are certain trends that are changing the way we look at physical rehabilitation. Changes in policy, both on the national and state level are expanding careers in physical therapy (increasing the number of administrative and doctor of physical therapy roles) and the industry as a whole. To understand these developments, we have to look at the history of the physical therapy industry and how physical therapist careers have evolved up until now.

Starting at the Beginning

During World War I (1917-1918), persons employed in hospitals and army rehabilitation camps to do rehabilitation work were called reconstruction aides. These aides were mostly women with working backgrounds in physical education at primary and secondary schools who participated in three-month-long courses run by physicians and nurses to train them in massage and muscle reeducation.

In 1921, the American Women's Physical Therapeutic Association (later called the American Physiotherapy Association) was founded by Mary McMillan (1880-1959), one of the pioneers of the physical therapy profession and the founding president of the American Physical Therapy Association. Born in Hyde Park, Massachusetts, and educated in England, she was the first physical therapy aide in World War I, where she oversaw the training of reconstruction aides and became known as "The Mother of Physical Therapy" in the U.S. Army. She also organized one of the first courses in physical therapy in the U.S., at Reed College in Oregon, and she established the first physical therapy training center in China at Peiping Union Medical College. Under her leadership, rehabilitation aides battled the raging polio epidemic that began in 1924 (it would last until 1956), and these nascent physical therapists worked hard to strengthen and rehabilitate victims.

By 1928, a council on physical therapy was established within the American Medical Association (AMA), and a standard for length of PT education was set at nine months. Education remained under the direction of the AMA until 1977. Physical therapy historians agree that physical therapy evolved as a professional field as a response to the polio epidemic, during which therapists worked in conjunction with physicians to battle the disease, reeducating weakened muscles through exercise and applying thermal hot packs to

Visit Vault at **www.vault.com** for insider company profiles, expert advice, career message boards, expert resume reviews, the Vault Job Board and more.

VAULT CAREER LIBRARY 17

painful joints. The polio epidemic in the United States would kill 6,000 people and paralyze 27,000 more; in the early 1950s there were still more than 20,000 cases each year until a vaccine (Salk's) proved successful in 1955.

In the 1960s, amendments to the Social Security Act that created Medicare and Medicaid necessitated an increase in physical therapy manpower. Persons over 65 were now able to receive physical therapy services in the acute care and outpatient setting through federal insurance (Medicare), so more people could afford them, and in turn, sought these services. Likewise, persons under the national poverty line received rehabilitation services through Medicaid, so more people previously unable to afford these services now wanted them. During this decade, the physical therapist assistant position was developed to help meet the growing needs of health care personnel.

In the 1970s, the APTA House of Delegates (a body of physical therapists representing each state in the American Physical Therapy Association) established standards for accreditation of all schools of physical therapy. Currently, there are 203 accredited schools of physical therapy in the United States, including one in Puerto Rico. All are accredited by the American Physical Therapy Association and therefore are subject to periodic quality review and evaluation by the Commission on Accreditation of Physical Therapy Education, an outside accrediting body that conducts periodic quality reviews of all existing physical therapists.

In the 1980s, the APTA upped the certification requirements for physical therapists to master's-level programs, thus transitioning the terminal degree for physical therapists from a baccalaureate to master's level. In the 1990s, the American Disabilities Act was signed mandating reasonable accommodation for all persons with disabilities and disease, increasing the need for physical therapists to prepare persons with disabilities for the workplace and to prepare and inform employers about the needs of disabled persons. The profession of physical therapy has continued to evolve and mature as a profession in response to the aging population, new epidemics such as AIDS and cancer, and the increasing incidence of head and spinal cord injury due to increased violence in urban areas. The profession has expanded its vision to include exercise as a form of disease prevention, continued to revise evaluation and treatment protocol for traditional patient populations such as those involving stroke and spinal cord injury, and continued to insure that practice techniques are based on evidence-based research as opposed to theory and common practice. The profession also continues to change in response to managed care and new reimbursement policies and procedures. The American Physical Therapy Association intends all states to be direct access (not requiring referral from a physician) states by the year 2010.

The Physical Therapy Industry Today

Now that we know the history of physical therapy careers, we can look at emerging industry trends, such as direct access, managed care and the effects of an aging population.

Direct access

Physical therapists may practice in a direct access state such as California and in this case may evaluate any patient without a physician referral. There are currently 39 states allow physical therapists direct access to patients without a referral from a physician: Alaska, Arizona, Arkansas, California, Colorado, Delaware, Florida, Idaho, Illinois, Iowa, Kentucky, Louisiana, Maine, Maryland, Massachusetts, Minnesota, Montana, Nebraska, Nevada, New Hampshire, New Jersey, New Mexico, North Carolina, North Dakota, Ohio, Oregon, Pennsylvania, Rhode Island, South Carolina, South Dakota, Tennessee, Texas, Utah, Vermont, Virginia, Washington, West Virginia, Wisconsin and Wyoming. However, the statutory language allowing direct access to treatment by the physical therapist is often ambiguous. The American Physical Therapy Association (APTA) claims that only 18 of the 39 states have clear language that allows direct treatment and four states have clear language allowing access only upon referral of a physician. The other 17 states have ambiguous language or do not talk about the topic at all.

Why is direct access such an important point of interest for the physical therapist and patient population? In a state like New York, which is as of yet not a direct access state, the PT may only evaluate and treat with a physician's referral, which will often read: "Evaluate and treat." Advocates of direct access see this step as superfluous and more a byproduct of doctors maintaining control over physical therapists than having any meaningful health implications for the patient. Proponents of direct access believe that physical therapists should be able to evaluate and treat patients based solely on patient complaint and need of services.

Advocates, who may be therapists, patients or their family members, see several overall advantages to direct access for the consumer. First, direct access saves money for both consumers and insurers. When a patient has to

Visit Vault at www.vault.com for insider company profiles, expert advice, career message boards, expert resume reviews, the Vault Job Board and more.

VAULT CAREER LIBRARY   19

go to a referring physician first, he must pay for the doctor's visit and the physical therapy visit. Secondly, direct access maintains a high quality of care because persons of all disabilities may choose from the entire pool of physical therapists. Third, direct access encourages preventive health care. By educating patients on how to avoid injury or illness, therapists potentially decrease the number of visits to the emergency room by state, saving costs on health care expenditure nationwide. Moreover, direct access makes physical therapy services more accessible to more people because if physicians (traditional first-contact providers) are in short supply in any geographic area, persons wishing to receive physical therapy in non-direct access states may have to wait for long periods of time, or not receive physical therapy at all.

One recent historical milestone for the physical therapy industry is the APTA's 2000 passing of the APTA Vision Statement, which aims to prepare physical therapists as doctors of physical therapy able to provide direct access to all patients in all states by 2020. Currently physical therapy educational programs nationwide are transitioning from master's-level to doctorate-level graduate programs, reflecting the industry's increasing emphasis on further education in the field. Therapists need to know how to make a functional diagnosis and prognosis, analyze evaluative data and develop treatment plans, all derived from research-based evidence. In addition, they need to continually add to the collective research data bank, and act as consultants and expert educators; all of these responsibilities demand a doctoral-level degree. In fact, the Commission on Accreditation in Physical Therapy Education (CAPTE) implemented a mandate over five years ago that the goal for physical therapy education programs and for physical therapy as a profession was to require a master's degree in physical therapy for all students studying to become physical therapists. All programs that did not comply with this mandate would lose accreditation status from CAPTE. All students look to enter programs accredited by CAPTE because they know that certain normative standards and quality education are required and evaluated by an ongoing auditing process.

But why did the physical therapy field move to demand higher education in the first place? Largely, physical therapists increasingly needed a curriculum that included research design, courses in quantitative and qualitative research methods, practice in research and statistics to remain competitive and competent in today's health care arena. To practice, physical therapists read literature steeped in research methodology and change or alter practice based on what has been proven empirically. The more recent initiative to require a doctoral degree by 2020 came about largely because more than half of the states in the U.S. have passed a direct access law that licenses physical therapists as autonomous practitioners with the ability to diagnose. Other diagnosticians, including physicians and psychologists, require doctoral degrees, and physical therapy aims to demand the same level of expertise.

An aging population

U.S. census estimates reflect that one in five persons in the United States has a disability and one in 10 has a severe disability. The U.S. is also an aging population: persons 65 and older are becoming the largest age group in the nation, requiring an increase in therapeutic services to manage functional limitations associated with both disease and the natural course of aging. Therefore, there is a continual demand for physical therapists to work on both the prevention and rehabilitation side of combating chronic disease associated with aging.

Wellness

A current trend in the industry is for physical therapists to become, and then stay, more involved in the "wellness" movement in health care. In other words, physical therapists are considered to have the most useful inside knowledge of how exercise can assist in improving quality of life, and they are finding themselves becoming increasingly vocal spokespersons and consultants in combating obesity/inactivity and its ramifications, often through preventative measures. Physical therapists work in elementary schools, health clubs, private businesses and rehabilitation centers to provide patients with exercise protocols and educational tools to prevent obesity.

Managed care

Physical therapists are also increasingly being called upon to go beyond mere physical therapy programs. PTs with at least five years of experience are leading rehabilitation units of nursing homes, rehabilitation centers and acute care hospitals throughout the United States. Managed care organizations, which began sprouting up in the 1980s to curb the escalating cost of American health care, provide a limited number of health care services to individuals, based on diagnosis; this change disabled many freestanding hospitals and other health care facilities from sustaining operation individually, and they were subsequently bought out and restructured by organizations such as Gentiva, Kessler and Health South. And these organizations now recruit for the recently developed role of director of rehabilitation (who oversees physical therapy, occupational therapy and speech therapy) from pools of physical therapists,

Visit Vault at **www.vault.com** for insider company profiles, expert advice, career message boards, expert resume reviews, the Vault Job Board and more.

V/\ULT CAREER LIBRARY   **21**

who are often sought for these roles because they have proven to have excellent time-management skills and their educational programs train them in leadership and administrative management. So there's ample room to climb a career ladder for those who wish to take on supervisory roles in rehab departments in acute care facilities throughout the United States. PTs are being called up to manage occupational therapy and speech therapy departments as well as their own units.

Medicare

Physical therapists nationwide are currently concerned with how Medicare regulations will change their reimbursement patterns. There is currently a moratorium on a Medicare Cap-federal legislation that was passed to reduce spending by consumers covered by Medicare and their providers. The Medicare Cap states that under Medicare Part B, patients can receive up to $1,740 in physical therapy and speech therapy combined and $1,740 in occupational therapy services. Some physical therapists are fighting the Medicare Cap, because they don't believe physical therapy services should be limited in order to save health care expenses nationally; they argue that each case is unique. For example, a therapist may be treating a breast cancer patient who is 73, and has pronounced edema and weakness in her involved arm. This patient, because of the Medicare Cap, is cut off from services before she has functional use of her arm. The therapist experiences firsthand the emotional and physical pain of the patient, and decides that the law is unfair. This therapist becomes a political advocate, joining a political action committee sponsored by the APTA to fight the Medicare Cap, because her direct experience has shown that those persons covered by Medicare are not able to receive all of the health services they need with the Medicare Cap in place. Across all states, physical therapists have joined political action committees to lobby against this cap; this cohesive action is an example of how physical therapists are becoming increasingly involved in political advocacy to protect the rights of patients and the field of physical therapy.

Code of Ethics

The physical therapy association has a distinct code of ethics. Established by the APTA, the code was a response to acknowledgment by the health care world that physical therapy was a legitimate, growing profession. As with other professional bodies that include role socialization (the process of learning what conduct is expected and maintained by one's colleagues), physical therapists began to need a script of moral conduct by which to abide, primarily because of the vast array of settings in which they found themselves working.

The code of ethics is taught in all schools of physical therapy, and students learn ethical standards through role-playing case studies in which those standards are maintained or breached. Some examples of ethical standards include patient confidentiality, not exploiting a patient's vulnerability, and trust and honesty in the patient/therapist relationship. Patient confidentiality is not only an ethical standard but the law. In 1996, Congress enacted the HIPPAA Health Insurance Portability and Accounting Act, which was published in April 2001 and enforced since April 2003 by the Office of Civil Rights. The primary purpose for the act was for continuance of health insurance coverage in changing jobs, but the Act also provided legal standards for the confidentiality and security of patient data. Not only must physical therapists be aware of holding patient's personal information in confidence verbally by not discussing cases in elevators and cafeterias, but physical therapists must be aware of the sensitivity of a patient's records; patients' signatures are needed for the release of any patient data to another health care provider. Other items in the physical therapy code of ethics are not matters of federal or state law, of course, but a set of moral guidelines, such as always speaking the truth and never harming a patient.

Research

As more physical therapists become involved in clinical research, for example examining how feasible an exercise program is for women with breast cancer who are still undergoing chemotherapy, or examining the effect of a weight-management program on obese children, it is essential that PTs become certified in the ethics of research. Most physical therapists are new researchers and need to be aware of the rights and responsibilities of subjects in their research. These include making sure all participants in a research program are aware of the purpose and significance of the research, know they can choose not to participate at any time, and sign a subject consent form. Health care facilities often have their own institutional review board (IRB) where research proposals must be approved.

Physical therapy educational programs around the nation have students participate in full research projects or research proposals, such as how Pilates exercise can improve the strength of abdominal muscles in patients with poor posture, or how a group exercise protocol can increase the functional use of an affected arm in women following a stroke, and orient these students to the mechanisms of the institutional review board process, whether that happens

Visit Vault at **www.vault.com** for insider company profiles, expert advice, career message boards, expert resume reviews, the Vault Job Board and more.

VΛULT CAREER LIBRARY   **23**

at a university or health care facility. In addition, the National Institutes of Health offers online courses to practicing physical therapists and other health professionals who are considering taking on a research project to become sufficiently knowledgeable about patient's rights and privacy issues.

GETTING HIRED

Education

Today, educational programs graduating physical therapists award either a Masters of Science or a Doctorate of Science. All physical therapy programs are at the graduate level and require a college degree. Depending on the number of required prerequisites, an individual can transfer from a BS or BA degree, length of educational programs range from two to four years.

An undergraduate degree (BS or BA) is a must for applying to graduate school in physical therapy. There is no specific major looked on more favorably than another in terms of preparation for graduate school in physical therapy, but students applying to physical therapy programs often have undergraduate degrees in psychology or sociology, which can benefit future health care professionals as they may be more attuned to the psychosocial issues of health care delivery. Remember that all physical therapy graduate programs will require a certain number of prerequisites, often including chemistry, anatomy and physiology, physics and statistics, but depending on requirements for undergraduate majors, a student applying to grad school may have one or more of the prerequisites already taken care of. PT educational programs generally include classes in the basic sciences, therapeutic sciences, liberal arts and research education.

Where to Go

There are many physical therapy schools (more than 200) in the nation accredited by the American Physical Therapy Association. A school without this accreditation (CAPTE) is not worth a grain of salt because the association has standards with which all educational programs must comply. Find out about specific programs through each school's web site. The American Physical Therapy Association is also a good source of information, as is the annual list of accredited physical therapist education programs in the U.S., Puerto Rico and Canada in the *Physical Therapy Journal*, which you can find in your local library.

The university and four-year colleges that currently have accredited programs are categorized in the appendix of this guide by state. All of these programs have unique strengths, but for the past 15 years, the following programs have been known as the best and the most competitive to get into: Boston University, Columbia University, Temple University, MGH Institute of Health, University of North Carolina at Chapel Hill and Emory University.

The University of Puerto Rico has an excellent program taught in Spanish. As in other professions, the reputation of the physical therapy school matters. For physical therapy, the school's passing rate on licensure exam, employability of alumni, reputation of faculty and age of program all factor in.

Programs differ in terms of class format; some are taught in the evening, some in the day and some on the weekend. Programs also differ in terms of whether they culminate in a master's or doctoral degree. Some programs admit women students only, such as Simmons College in Massachusetts and Texas Woman's University; most programs allow transfer students, but transferred courses are weighed individually by each university admissions department; some are housed within a medical school and some are not. Other considerations you'll want to keep in mind include the geographic area, financial aid and scholarship availability, the size of the faculty, the relationship with the local community, cost of the program and faculty to student ratio.

To learn more about a college/university that houses a particular program, a *Barrons* or *Peterson's Graduate School Guide* may be the best way to go. Do know that all programs have similar high standards for grade point averages (generally 3.3 or above) and also look for excellent references, great presentation at the interview (may be an on-site or phone interview), examples of interest in participating in community health projects, and evidence that you've explored the field and are knowledgeable about what physical therapists do.

Admissions and Cost

In the mid-1990s there were more applicants to PT schools than there were spots available. Schools could be choosy. Admissions were highly competitive. Since then, PT educational programs have proliferated, and schools now have to market their programs in order to recruit applicants. Most programs leading to an entry-level degree in physical therapy are full time, but programs are cognizant of the possibility that students need to work while going to school and offer flexible class and time schedules. Weekend programs hold classes Fridays to Sundays to allow students to continue to hold jobs while going to school. Students graduating from either a master's- or doctoral-level program must sit for a state licensing exam currently offered in written format only. Many educational programs encourage students to attend an exam preparatory course held at various locations throughout the U.S. in order to prepare for this challenging test.

Physical therapy programs are quite costly to attend. The average cost of a professional program (two years for master's, three years for doctoral) is $54,083.25. The tuition is worth the investment, however, as the median salary reported by the PTA is $52,000 based on a 2,644 response survey (Redman-Bentley, 2004). Do know that this is a median national salary and that salaries range widely based on urban and rural areas. (Hiring bonuses are sometimes offered to attract graduates to rural areas.)

Hands-On Training

In addition to your GPA and class rank, PT programs and employers want to see hands-on experience in your application. By looking at your volunteer work, PT aide experience and internships, employers and schools can see that you are committed to a career that depends so much on one-on-one interaction.

If you are interested in applying to graduate school in physical therapy, get some real-life experience (volunteer or paid) as a physical therapy aide in a hospital, health club, nursing home or school. You'll see firsthand what the physical therapist does and show that this experience has fueled your motivation to apply to graduate school and become a physical therapist.

Volunteer work and PT aides

Many schools look favorably on the fact that an applicant has done either volunteer work as a physical therapy aide or worked as a physical therapy aide before applying to physical therapy school. To get a physical therapy aide job, look in the classifieds of your area newspapers under physical therapy aide for openings, and when applying make sure you mention that you are also applying to physical therapy school—facilities also look favorably upon applicants who have a real commitment to the profession. If your local newspaper does not have listings, call the physical therapy department directors in your neighboring health care facilities, and inquire about aide openings. Some graduate schools of physical therapy accept a number of physical therapist assistants who have obtained the required prerequisites to apply for graduate school. (A PTA does not have to take physics, organic chemistry and other undergraduate courses to become a

Visit Vault at **www.vault.com** for insider company profiles, expert advice, career message boards, expert resume reviews, the Vault Job Board and more.

VAULT CAREER LIBRARY   29

PTA. If a PTA decides to go on and become a PT, he'll have to take additional courses before applying to graduate school.)

Experience as a physical therapist assistant isn't necessary for applying to graduate school in physical therapy, although some schools consider that a strength in terms of criteria for application. And remember that there is a difference between a physical therapy aide and a physical therapist assistant!

Internships

Internships (for master's degree) such as a five-week experience treating orthopedic injuries at Columbia Presbyterian in New York or a six-week experience treating children with developmental disabilities at a public school in North Carolina, or residencies (for the DPT degree) are usually three to five in number and range from a total of 24 weeks to one year. An internship or clinical affiliation course is defined as a practical hands-on experience of six to 10 weeks in length, in which the student is assigned to a hospital or outpatient facility with a supervisor at the site (a physical therapist). The student will practice learned skills in this supervised real environment to better prepare him for entry-level physical therapy.

The Hiring Process

CHAPTER 5

With so many different physical therapy jobs out there, it is easy to find one that's right for you and apply for it.

Professors and directors in the educational programs often have notices of jobs available and refer students to companies/hospitals, etc. In addition, many physical therapists get hired for open positions available at the company for which they've previously interned. Many companies prefer to hire these students as full-time employees, since they've already had the opportunity to evaluate the quality of their work.

To become a licensed physical therapist, students graduating from a physical therapy program must sit for a state licensing exam and achieve an 80 percent pass rate. You'll also need a flawless resume, interview and reference bank. You must have good references. Your background will be checked and investigated. Your internship supervisors, colleagues and co-workers can be references for you. Educational programs often assist their students in skills that increase likelihood of landing the best job possible.

Cover Letter and Resume Advice

Prospective employers will read your cover letter and resume before they ever meet you. This means that your cover letter and resume can be the make-or-break parts of your application that get your foot in the door of the PT industry.

Cover letter

Cover letters should be no more than one page long. They are generally three paragraphs long. You should tailor the letter, so that your skills match the requirement of the job you're applying for.

The first paragraph should be an introduction, where you state that you are writing (to the person named in the ad, or if no person is named, then "Dear Sir or Madam,") to express your interest in the position (typing the correct title of the position), at the particular company. State where you saw the position advertised. Then, offer a brief introduction of why you think you would make an excellent candidate for the position. Focus on how you have the skills the company is looking for.

The second paragraph should expand upon your introduction, highlighting the particular skills mentioned in the job ad, and illustrating examples that demonstrate that you possess those skills. For example, if the job ad states the company wants a "well-organized, detail-oriented person with good communication skills," give specific examples illustrating how you are well organized, detail oriented, and you have good communication skills. State that you feel these experiences and qualifications make you an excellent candidate for the position at this company. For example, "I worked in a hospital, where I managed a case load of 90 patients, so this exemplifies my organization skills."

The last paragraph should state how you look forward to an opportunity to meet with the contact person to discuss your experiences and qualifications. Reiterate your phone number, and state that you have attached your resume to the letter. Close with: "Thank you for your attention and consideration."

Resume

Most resumes should be kept to one page. They should list your education, certifications/licenses and prior work experience (including internships). Your work experience should highlight the duties that you have performed, using "action words," (such as led, performed, provided, supervised). If you have special skills (for example, if you are bilingual), those should be featured on the resume. You should also list skills and special talents that are likely to make your resume seem unique and appealing to the person reading it (for example, if you developed and led a support group, developed or created a research project, or presented a paper at a conference). It is also helpful to list areas in which you may have had supervisory responsibility. Keep it clear, simple and easy to read. Use a plain font, black color for the typeface and white, high quality paper if submitting by mail, though most facilities currently would rather accept resumes electronically as an attachment. Also, proofread and spell-check any document you send to an employer. The online *PT Bulletin* and online *ADVANCE* magazine are good sources for browsing jobs available in physical therapy.

Resume design depends on the health care facility site and the applicant's previous experience. Typical design and pertinent content for a recent graduate is conveyed on the following page. It is important that resumes for the hospital setting are kept short; usually one page suffices. The objective should be clear. If the applicant has bilingual skills this should be included in bold as this is seen as an important asset by all potential employers. Note: it is important that all recent physical therapy graduates have the means to send a resume electronically to a potential employer. Most human resource departments prefer electronic versions of resumes.

Resume Template

Name

PT State Licensure Number

Contact information, including e-mail, home phone, work phone, cell phone.

OBJECTIVE
(E.g., "To work in a challenging environment where I can employ my skills as a physical therapist.")

DATE:

EXPERIENCE:

EDUCATION:

CONTINUING EDUCATION COURSES:

EXPERIENCE GAINED ON CLINICAL AFFILIATIONS OR RESIDENCIES:

REFERENCES:

SPECIAL AWARDS OR MERIT SCHOLARSHIPS:

MEMBER ORGANIZATIONS:

Visit Vault at **www.vault.com** for insider company profiles, expert advice, career message boards, expert resume reviews, the Vault Job Board and more.

VAULT CAREER LIBRARY   33

Sample Resume

Anna Ortiz, PT, MS

Annaortiz@hotmail.com

EDUCATION

Texas Women's University-Houston: MS in Physical Therapy
University of Rochester: BA in Psychology

AWARDS

First place student research award, Texas Regional Chapter of the American
College of Sports Medicine

Clinical Experience

Ben Hogan Sports Therapy Institute	2003-2006
Physical Therapist	
Gentiva Orthopedics	2001-2003
Physical Therapist	
Health South	1999-2001
Physical Therapist	

PUBLICATIONS

Ortiz, A., Core Stability in the Female Athlete. PT Journal, December 2002.

PRESENTATIONS

2003 Texas Regional Chapter of the American College of Sports Medicine:
"Reliability of Selected Physical Performance Tests in Adult Young Women."

LANGUAGES

English and Spanish

MEMBERSHIPS

American Physical Therapy Association
International Federation of Sports Medicine
American College of Sports Medicine

The Interview

The kind of interview a person may have depends less on the setting (acute care, sports, etc.) than it does on the size of the institution. A larger institution may require a longer interview process as the applicant meets with more than one level of management hierarchy.

The interview process usually consists of at least two interviews, with the persons who will be your supervisors, as well as with an HR person. Also, ideally, you would want to see the facility, program or area where you will work to get a sense of how you would feel working in that location.

General interview questions

Generally, the interview questions are posed to determine whether you've done your own research about the institution/center that you're applying to; whether you're able to self-reflect and recognize areas of strength and areas for personal improvement; and whether you feel confident enough with background information and content of the educational program to begin entry-level work. The interview may also include a request for applicants to do a PowerPoint presentation on an aspect of physical therapy they are interested in.

Interview questions can also vary depending on the site for potential employment. If an applicant seeks work at a skilled nursing facility (nursing home), questions may include, "What is your reason for wanting to work with older adults?" An applicant who states that she is primarily interested in working with orthopedic problems throughout the age-span may be asked how her specific interest in orthopedics evolved. If you're looking for your first job as a physical therapist, you will want to convey to potential employers your interest first in gaining experience as a generalist (treating all patient populations) and later specifically concentrating on one patient population group.

A physical therapy interview often starts like any other interview, with general questions. Here are some possible opening questions:

"Tell me about yourself" is often asked. This is an opportunity to state where you went to school, a brief description of your internship or experience and why you want to work for the company. Do not go into too much detail.

Visit Vault at **www.vault.com** for insider company profiles, expert advice, career message boards, expert resume reviews, the Vault Job Board and more.

VAULT CAREER LIBRARY   35

"Why do you want to work here?" This is an opportunity to explain what you know about the company and the position, and why you feel you are the best candidate for this position.

"What are your strengths/what are your weaknesses?" List at least three positive qualities (for example, you are organized, dedicated, hardworking) and for the weakness, list one quality that can be considered a positive attribute (for example, "I am a perfectionist," and explain how this is so).

"Where do you see yourself in five years?" The interviewer wants to find out how long you will stay with the company. You can decide how you want to express this, but essentially the goal is to say something that shows you do not plan to quit six months from now. Show that your goals fit in with those of the company. For example, if the company has room for advancement, you can state that you hope to see yourself in a supervisory position. Some interviewers may ask prospective employees what their long- and short-term goals are. To answer with the right amount of self-reflection and accuracy, know the hierarchy of the company, the opportunity for continuing education within the company and funding for internal and external coursework, and realistically assess your own expectations. Depending on their own strengths and desires, physical therapists may decide to conduct research and try to publish clinical studies, they may decide to become a board-certified clinical specialist, they may decide that they want to go into teaching. All answers indicate a physical therapist who is a lifelong learner, which is a quality valued by the profession as a whole. A physical therapist who wants to project herself as a team member may state that after 10 years of clinical work as a physical therapist, she would like to manage an interdisciplinary department of rehabilitation specialists.

Case examples

You will almost always be asked about a case example. Be prepared to describe specific client cases in detail. You will often be asked about how you managed a difficult case, to illustrate how you work under pressure or handle difficult situations. Explain how you managed the difficulty, showing your teamwork or communication skills. Always present this issue in the most positive light. Never say anything to make yourself seem as though you cannot get along with others. You want to present yourself as someone who works well with others.

Sample Interview Questions and Answers

In addition to the questions below, your interviewer may ask questions that test knowledge learned in PT school, but these are less common. Here are some sample commonly asked questions and possible responses:

1. How did you first become interested in physical therapy?

Possible answer: "I first became interested in physical therapy when my grandmother suffered a stroke and I observed what went on in her physical therapy sessions. I was impressed by the caring, intelligent and professional way in which my grandmother was handled."

2. What do you feel were your strengths as a physical therapy student and what were your weaknesses?

Possible answer: "My strengths included my ability to work independently on my research project and assist others in planning how to develop a good research proposal. I would also cite my time-management abilities as a strength, as well as my ability to balance my love of exercise and community activities with the demands of the program. My weakness was that I spent less time on the courses I felt were not where I wanted to concentrate as a physical therapist, not realizing at the time that my areas of specialization would only crystallize once I was in the field."

3. What are you most excited about when thinking about potentially working at our institution?

Possible answer: "I am thrilled that this is a teaching institution and I will be among experts in the medical and rehabilitation field. I will be able to attend inservices, case conferences with people who have had much experience in treatment and research. I am also excited that this is an institution in my own community, and therefore I will be a provider of physical therapy for a community I love and am familiar with."

4. What are you most concerned about when thinking about potentially working at our institution?

Possible answer: "It is a busy place and patient load demands will be challenging, but I am sure I will be able to handle it."

Visit Vault at **www.vault.com** for insider company profiles, expert advice, career message boards, expert resume reviews, the Vault Job Board and more.

VAULT CAREER LIBRARY

37

5. What is your style for facing conflicts? Do you prefer to solve problems by yourself, or in collaboration with others?

Possible answer: "I prefer to collaborate with peers and supervisors; however, I recognize that emergency situations require thinking on your feet and making an independent judgment, and I have the confidence to do that."

6. Imagine that you are on your first week of the job. You are ambulating (providing gait training) with a stroke patient and the patient falls and cannot get up alone. She is in pain and refuses to get up. What would you do in this situation?

Possible answer: "I would stay with the patient and ask a peer to call for the physician. Afterwards, I would write out an incident report regardless of the level of injury."

7. Imagine that you are in an elevator and a colleague is discussing a patient with you. The colleague is your superior but you feel the discussion is not appropriate for the elevator. What would you do in this situation?

Possible answer: "I would ask my colleague to refrain from discussing this in the elevator, as the confidentiality of the patient was being jeopardized."

In this case, the interviewer is looking to see how you respond in a crisis, whether you have ideas of who to go to in this case, whether you are concerned about your own liability or the safety of the patient.

ON THE JOB

Career Paths

Career paths for the physical therapist can vary greatly, as physical therapists have many diverse opportunities for carving their own specializations or niches within the profession.

Included in this chapter are some examples of the different paths you might take as a PT. Of course, none of these tracks are written in stone. A person practicing as a physical therapist may combine any number of areas of interest and job possibilities to make her career as interesting and lucrative as possible.

PTs always have the personal satisfaction of knowing they are helping other people with their problems; with a career in physical therapy comes the opportunity to literally change the course of someone's life for the better. Teaching people new ways to cope with problems, giving them new life skills they can use and advocating for clients can be very rewarding. It can be very fulfilling to work with people, as opposed to working with machines or inanimate objects. PTs can witness the results of their work, over time. And physical therapists tend to enjoy a healthy degree of economic satisfaction as well.

On the flip side, it can be overwhelming at times to work with persons who are in great pain and whose abilities have been diminished by illness or disease. You will learn from experience how to give compassion and time to your patients, while maintaining the boundaries between work and home. The physical therapy profession demands a lot of energy, and recharging, the ability to focus on things outside of work in order to start each day anew, is essential.

The Acute Care Track

In school, you noticed that you really enjoyed courses and topics related to acute care and pediatrics. You decide to apply to an acute care hospital that has a pediatric unit to gain general practice experience and see if you continue to enjoy the pediatric population. After working at the acute care hospital for three years, you decide to apply to a hospital that concentrates solely in pediatrics, such as Children's Hospital in Boston, Mass. After five years there, you apply for an adjunct teaching position specializing in pediatrics at your regional university. You find that the combination of staying current in

Visit Vault at **www.vault.com** for insider company profiles, expert advice, career message boards, expert resume reviews, the Vault Job Board and more.

VAULT CAREER LIBRARY   41

the field by working at a pediatric acute care hospital and adjunct teaching in pediatrics is the perfect fit.

One example of a typical career path is as follows. Susan B. graduates from an accredited physical therapy program. She accepts a job at an urban acute care hospital and gains experience with a variety of patient diagnoses by rotating in different areas in the hospital. She decides that she is very interested in evaluating and treating cancer patients (or another specialty). She looks for jobs working with this patient group. She moves up to administrator, still treating patients and may move then to teaching, research or stay active in patient care.

Uppers and downers

Uppers: High salary and sound benefits, the potential to gain much experience, and fast-paced if you like that. If the setting is a teaching hospital, there is much opportunity for interdisciplinary learning, room to grow professionally and be promoted to higher position.

Downers: Patients can be very sick and therefore very demanding emotionally. Some people find the setting depressing. If you don't like to work with hierarchy, you won't like acute care because there is a long chain of command.

The Rehabilitation Track

In physical therapy school, you greatly enjoyed courses in neurology and rehabilitation. After graduating, you applied to an outpatient rehabilitation center focusing on neurological injuries. You worked there for three years treating persons with stroke, spinal cord injury, multiple sclerosis and Parkinson's disease. You were promoted to director of the PT department. You decide that neurological rehabilitation and administration is your niche, and remain in this position for five years. You then apply for a position as rehabilitation director at a renowned rehabilitation facility and oversee not only physical therapists but also speech therapists and occupational therapists. Alternatively, you might have decided to begin to teach part time and obtain your doctoral degree in education in order to apply for a full-time faculty job. You could then become certified in neurodevelopmental technique and teach continuing education courses on a national circuit.

Or, let's say you greatly enjoyed orthopedics and sports physical therapy. After graduating, you applied to an outpatient rehabilitation center focusing on musculoskeletal injuries. You worked there for three years and then applied for a job with a professional sports team as their personal physical therapist. You worked there for five years, gained an excellent reputation in your community and opened up a private practice for musculoskeletal and sports injuries.

Uppers and downers

Uppers: More time with your patients and therefore more time to practice techniques learned in school. Also, you'll have the chance to work closely with occupational and speech therapists to plan treatment for patients, as well as possibly seeing patients become functionally independent, because, unlike the acute care setting, you may see a patient for one to three months.

Downers: Slower-paced, if you prefer fast-paced environments like the acute care unit.

Fitness Centers

In school, you enjoyed learning about sports physical therapy and how exercise can be used to promote healthy lifestyles for persons across the age span. You were a dancer before applying to physical therapy school and now have decided that on graduation you will work in a fitness center developing exercise programs for persons with disabilities. You begin in an Equinox health club located on the Upper West Side of New York and become trusted for your creative combination of manual therapy and exercise. You are promoted to assistant manager of the clinic and stay there for 10 years, advocating for continual remodeling of the facility to facilitate the use of this Equinox center and others for persons with disabilities.

Or, let's say you enjoyed learning about how physical therapists are staying on the cutting edge of rehabilitation, becoming informed about the benefits of different exercise programs and treatment procedures such as Pilates, Tai Chi and acupuncture. You decide on graduation you will work in rehabilitation with persons in the performing arts. You begin in an outpatient center in an urban area catering to this population and stay there for 10 years before moving and opening up your own clinic with advice from your mentor.

Visit Vault at **www.vault.com** for insider company profiles, expert advice, career message boards, expert resume reviews, the Vault Job Board and more.

V/\ULT CAREER LIBRARY   **43**

Uppers and downers

Uppers: You are working with both the able and disabled population and may find the setting more upbeat and optimistic.

Downers: Not as much potential for growth.

Nursing Homes

While in school, you noticed that you enjoyed learning about and working with the older adult population. You decided upon graduation that you would try working in a nursing home to see if you could make a difference in older people's lives. You worked in the nursing home for four years, were promoted to supervisor and then to director of rehabilitation. You decided to go back to school at night, to get an MBA to assist you in your new responsibilities. You were consistently invited to provide courses in PT by the APTA and national physical therapy educational program for the older adult and became an advocate for the older adult in both local and federal organizations. Later you run for an APTA office, becoming well known in your field.

Uppers and downers

Uppers: Chance to work with the older adult population if you like that.

Downers: Can be depressing, as persons do not improve enough to go home and sometimes die at the center.

Schools

While in school, you enjoyed learning rehabilitation techniques for children with disabilities. You are married with three children and know that you want to find a job that offers flexibility for you to be home on holidays and in the summer. You decide to apply to the Board of Education in New York City as a school physical therapist. You evaluate and treat children in schools for four years, and as it fits perfectly with your lifestyle decide to remain with this position and add a part-time private practice for children with neurological disabilities.

Here's another example. Albert Perez graduates from an accredited physical therapy program and starts to work for the Board of Education. He works a five-day week at P.S. 87 in New York City for nine months and gets summers off and great benefits. He may even have his schooling paid by the Board of Education if he commits to one year of working. After four years with Board of Ed., he decides he wants to try to get into academia because he feels he presents well at conferences. He applies for a job as an adjunct specializing in pediatric PT and goes on to try to apply for a full-time job at his local college. He gets the job and goes on to get his PhD.

Uppers and downers

Uppers: Chance to work with children; flexible schedules with good pay.

Downers: Less of a chance to go to inservices and trainings, as at an acute care hospital.

Private Practice

While in school, you envision yourself as having your own private practice. You know that you will first have to gain some experience in an acute care hospital or rehabilitation center before venturing on your own. Your first job is at Beth Israel Hospital and you gain general experience there for three years. You then choose to apply to an orthopedic outpatient center to gain experience in evaluation and treatment of musculoskeletal injuries. Following this experience, you and a peer decide to try to open your own private practice after securing initial funding from a relative. Your private practice is slow for the first year, but then your reputation for one-on-one treatment with your clients for 45 minutes to one hour becomes well known and you have very little competition. Your private practice becomes quite lucrative and you enjoy the autonomy.

Alternatively, let's say in school, you participated in a research project about the effect of exercise on persons recovering from prostate cancer. You decide to commit yourself to working with cancer patients and apply for a job at a nationally renowned cancer clinic (i.e., Sloan Kettering in N.Y.). You work there for five years and are promoted to supervisor of your department. You then open your own private practice treating only cancer patients.

Visit Vault at **www.vault.com** for insider company profiles, expert advice, career message boards, expert resume reviews, the Vault Job Board and more.

V∧ULT CAREER LIBRARY   **45**

Uppers and downers

Uppers: You'll have autonomy, and the chance to earn a lot of money.

Downers: You'll also have overwhelming responsibility, plus less flexibility in your work schedule unless the practice grows substantially and you can hire help.

A Day in the Life

CHAPTER 7

Generally speaking, there is no "typical day" for a physical therapist, since career paths and daily routines vary so widely. After two or three years of general practice, a physical therapist may find a special area of interest and devote energy and training to a specific patient population or specific treatment technique. For example, a physical therapist in Reno, Nevada, may find that his special area of interest is prevention of injuries in high school students involved in team sports and he may set up a private practice teaching adolescents and adults stretching and strengthening techniques and conditioning routines. A physical therapist living in New York City may have found her niche in evaluating and treating women living with breast cancer after total mastectomy procedures.

A day in the life of an entry-level physical therapist at an acute care hospital in a city will consist of seeing an assigned patient load that can range from eight to 12 patients a day in a quality facility. Too many patients a day equals an understaffed facility and compromises on care. Treatment times range from 20 minutes to 40 minutes, a much shorter time frame compared to the days before managed care, when typical treatment lasted 40 minutes to an hour. A physical therapist conducts her evaluations, treats her patients, documents all treatments (often written documentation can take 20 to 30 percent of the workday), attends inservices, which are educational training sessions for physical therapists by in-house and outside experts, and participates in interdisciplinary meetings. Physical therapy work is physically demanding, as therapists must use their own strength to transfer, gait train and exercise patients, and the new physical therapist will have to learn how to economize her own physical energy by scheduling time to document notes or other nonphysically demanding activity in between exercise sessions.

It is important for an individual pursuing the field of physical therapy to understand how wide the opportunities for practice in the field are. There is ALWAYS more to learn.

A Day in the Life:
Outpatient Rehabilitation

Cara Mateo works in an outpatient rehabilitation center in New York City that treats stroke patients, head injury, spinal cord injury, multiple sclerosis, Parkinson's and other neurological diseases. Cara is one of five other physical therapists working in her department. She reports directly to the director of physical therapy, who reports to the director of rehabilitation. Cara has been working at the rehabilitation center for two years.

7:30 a.m. Cara walks from her Upper West Side apartment to her job to arrive at 8:00. Her work day begins at 8:30 but she would like time to review her patient load and have a cup of coffee at her desk.

8:30 a.m. Cara has reviewed her e-mails, phone messages and schedule for the day. She attends an interdisciplinary care meeting with the rehabilitation team from 8:30 to 9:30 to review two problem cases.

9:30 a.m. Cara's first patient is called over the loudspeaker by the receptionist and Cara goes to the lobby area to receive her patient. He is a post-stroke patient and is wheelchair bound. He is accompanied by his wife. Cara works with her patient in "gait training" or walking with a quad cane (a cane with four prongs). Her patient is excited about his progress in terms of the distance he can accomplish. Cara suggests that in another two weeks she may progress him to a straight cane. Cara sits with her patient and his wife after the gait training to perform stretches on his upper extremity (arm) that have become tightened in a pattern typical of a stroke (called a synergy pattern). The three, therapist, wife and patient, work as a team to review home exercises. The session ends at 10:30.

10:30 a.m. Cara documents treatment in the patient's chart and includes reports of pain by the patient or reports of difficulty performing the exercise program. Cara also includes all exercises and gait training that she performed with the patient. She concludes her documentation with goals for the next treatment and a plan to carry these goals out.

Cara's second patient is called. This patient has multiple sclerosis and is also overweight. Cara's challenge, and the patient's, is to increase the patient's aerobic endurance without causing a relapse of fatigue (termed an exacerbation of symptoms cycle) typical of this condition. Cara checks the patient's vital signs, including blood pressure, heart rate and temperature. She also checks the patient's weight. Cara supervises the patient on aerobic circuit training, which includes the stationary bike, treadmill and upper body ergonometer. The patient is able to tolerate 15 minutes on each piece of equipment. Cara and the patient talk about when in the patient's day she feels most fatigued and what she does to alleviate this fatigue. Cara notes that the patient is wearing too much heavy clothing for the temperature of the gym and advises her about the effect of heat on the fatigue patterns of MS patients. Together they review the home exercise program. Cara walks her patient to the reception area after reviewing the next appointment time.

11:45 a.m. Cara documents the treatment of the MS patient.

12:00 p.m. Cara attends an interdepartmental inservice given by the director of the psychology department on cognitive deficits in stroke patients.

1:00 p.m. Cara sees her third patient of the day, a spinal cord-injured patient, aged 25. Her goals for this patient are to improve the patient's ability to move from the wheelchair to the mat and to increase his abdominal strength using the Bobath Ball (large gymnasium ball) for core (trunk) exercises. After a vigorous treatment, Cara and her patient talk about the fact that her patient would like to go back to work at some point. Cara makes a note that she will talk to the rehab team about a referral to the vocational department for training to return to work.

2:00 p.m. Cara documents her treatment.

2:15 p.m. Cara has an hour staff meeting to talk about the schedule for accepting PT students for the year from neighboring educational programs. The director would like to assign these students to a therapist. This is Cara's first time supervising a student and she is looking forward to the experience. Cara receives her assignment for a student from NYU.

3:15 p.m. Cara leads a group therapy session consisting of five post-stroke patients. The patients and Cara go through a series of exercises to improve balance. Cara has integrated some Tai Chi techniques into her group session and the patients enjoy this very much.

4:15 p.m. Cara documents the group therapy session in all five patient charts.

Visit Vault at **www.vault.com** for insider company profiles, expert advice, career message boards, expert resume reviews, the Vault Job Board and more.

VAULT CAREER LIBRARY

49

4:30 p.m. Cara reviews e-mails, phone calls that she received during the day and gets ready to leave for the day.

A Day in the Life:
Hospital, General Rotation

Kelly McGuinness is a senior physical therapist at Columbia Presbyterian Hospital in New York City. She has worked at this busy urban hospital since graduating from Columbia four years prior. She has had experience in all four general rotations: cardiopulmonary, neurology, orthopedics and pediatrics, and also spent six months on the breast cancer unit. She found that treating breast cancer patients following their mastectomies or lumpectomies was very satisfying and interesting to her. She was promoted to senior physical therapist of this unit.

7:30 a.m. Kelly arrives at the hospital to review the schedules of the four physical therapists that she supervises as well as to go over her own part-time case load.

8:00 a.m. Kelly has a breakfast meeting with her team, and they discuss any clinical problems that came up the day before. Kelly notes that one of her therapists is out sick, so she'll have to fill in for her on this day.

9:00 a.m. Kelly attends a physical therapy treatment with one of the therapists and offers advice on how to decrease inflammation in the patient's affected arm.

9:30 a.m. Kelly sees one of her own patients. She talks to her for 15 minutes about how to manage the pain the patient is feeling in her affected side. The patient describes the pain "as electrical shocks going down my arm—when I go to touch my arm I don't feel anything, I guess the sensation is gone." Kelly explains that during surgery nerve pathways were severed and the painful sensation can be partially alleviated by thermal (hot/cold therapy). Kelly provides this therapy for the patient in addition to passive and active stretching exercises for her involved arm and general conditioning exercises for post-surgery patients.

10:30 a.m. Kelly takes an hour in her office to answer e-mail and correspondence. Specifically, Kelly takes time to continue writing an application for an NIH grant to explore the effectiveness of two manual therapy techniques on arm pain post-mastectomy.

11:30 a.m. Kelly goes to an inservice presented by a hospital surgeon for all staff in the breast cancer unit.

12:30 p.m. Kelly eats at her desk and interviews a potential applicant for a new position.

1:30 p.m. Kelly sees three patients in a row and provides basic education for reducing swelling post-mastectomy, strengthening and stretching exercises, and resources for the patient to use once discharged to home, such as where to shop for prosthetics, various support groups for recovering breast cancer patients and health clubs in the community where patients can continue to exercise.

4:40 p.m. Kelly catches up on all paperwork and administrative duties. She returns all phone calls and leaves for home at 6:00 p.m.

Visit Vault at **www.vault.com** for insider company profiles, expert advice, career message boards, expert resume reviews, the Vault Job Board and more.

VAULT CAREER LIBRARY   **51**

Losing sleep over your job search?
Endlessly revising your resume?
Facing a work-related dilemma?

Super-charge your career with Vault's newest career tools: Resume Reviews, Resume Writing and Career Coaching.

Vault Resume Writing

On average, a hiring manager weeds through 120 resumes for a single job opening. Let our experts write your resume from scratch to make sure it stands out.

- Start with an e-mailed history and 1- to 2-hour phone discussion
- Vault experts will create a first draft
- After feedback and discussion, Vault experts will deliver a final draft, ready for submission

Vault Resume Review

- Submit your resume online
- Receive an in-depth e-mailed critique with suggestions on revisions within TWO BUSINESS DAYS

Vault Career Coach

Whether you are facing a major career change or dealing with a workplace dilemma, our experts can help you make the most educated decision via telephone counseling sessions.

- Sessions are 45-minutes over the telephone

For more information go to
www.vault.com/careercoach

V∧ULT
> the most trusted name in career information™

Final Analysis

CHAPTER 8

If you're strongly considering becoming a physical therapist, it's important to reflect on the following questions. Firstly, are you committed to attending an academically rigorous program? Physical therapy programs require a high GPA for acceptance and high academic standards are required during matriculation. Do you have the will and strong desire to be in a helping profession? Your first commitment is always to your patients. Do you want to become a health care professional and abide the ethics, rules and regulations and collective identity involved in this process? And finally, are you a team player?

In addition to these personality questions, you also have to ask yourself what kind of lifestyle you want to have. What kind of hours do you want? Salary? In this chapter, we will give you the lowdown on PT lifestyles.

Demographics

The physical therapist lives comfortably as jobs are plentiful, hours variable and the PT can often adjust her job to her current stage of life development.

Women make up the predominant majority of those who enter the field; women were not allowed into the medical profession for many years, seeking entry through nursing, physical and occupational therapy, and this history is still reflected today. Educational programs now have marketing forces to attract men and minorities to the workforce. Currently, there are programs, such as those spearheaded by the APTA's Foundation for Physical Therapy, in place to attract persons of diverse racial and cultural backgrounds into the field. The profession, and specifically the American Physical Therapy Association, recognizes that the profession will become stronger if there is a more balanced representation of men and women, as well as a more balanced representation of all races and cultural backgrounds. As patient demographics in the U.S. change, for example, as the Spanish-speaking patient population continues to grow, so must the demographics of health care providers including PTs. The Foundation for Physical Therapy, a fundraising organization under the APTA umbrella, offers several scholarship opportunities for minorities to attend graduate school (see the appendix for relevant web sites).

Salaries

Therapist salaries vary according to position, location, experience, type and size of hospital or employing agency. Therapists with little or no experience can earn between $40,000 and $60,000 per year. Annual salaries for experienced therapists range from $60,000 to $85,000, so salaries are largely dependent upon the worker's length of experience. The normal workweek is 40 hours, but these may include weekend appointments. Part-time work is also usually available. Therapists may also decide to work per diem, in which an employment agency will contract them out to hospitals and centers who hire for per diem work. Per diem therapists often receive insurance benefits from the employment agency and receive high hourly pay from their placement agency. Physical therapists who go on to teach in colleges and universities will be paid from $50,000 to $80,000 depending on their degree, scholarship and teaching experience. Physical therapists sometimes earn over $100,000 per year if they combine two jobs, such as a full-time position at an acute care hospital and home care practice on the weekends. Most employers provide fringe benefits such as paid vacations, sick leave, hospital and group insurance, and retirement programs.

APPENDIX

Glossary

Acupressure: manual pressure at pinpointed area of skin directly above the origin or insertion of a muscle in order to reduce tension and pain.

Acute care: hospital care aimed toward taking care of the initial phase of medical treatment immediately after persons are injured or diagnosed.

Aerobic: endurance exercise such as running walking, swimming. Lasts for 15 minutes or more.

Anaerobic: short-burst exercise lasting from zero to 15 minutes, such as sprints, bench presses, high jumps.

Cardiovascular: pertaining to the heart, arteries, veins and capillaries.

Contraindication: something that is not helpful but rather hurtful to the current condition or treatment. For instance, applying moist heat to a multiple sclerosis patient is contraindicated because heat increases fatigue in MS patients.

Craniosacral therapy: uses manual techniques to adjust the cranium and sacrum (bone below coccyx) to achieve pain-relieving effects throughout the body.

Direct access: patients can access the services of physical therapists without a physician's referral in some states.

Effleurage: wide sweeping motions of massage over entire body to increase circulation and relax muscles.

Friction massage: massage over a small surface area perpendicular to alignment of muscle fibers to reduce pain and increase circulation.

Gait training: ambulation (walking) practice by a physical therapist for persons recovering from orthopedic or neurological injury.

Inservices: educational sessions at hospitals and health care facilities given to train or inform staff and maintain currency in practice and motivate staff to keep learning.

Interdisciplinary team: team of professionals from different disciplines; for example, a physical therapist, occupational therapist and social worker with a physician make an interdisciplinary team. There can be other combinations.

Manual therapy: any certified physical therapy treatment that involves the hands.

Mobilization: simply means to move tissues to produce an effect.

Modality: a physical therapy treatment that uses heat, ultrasound, electricity, traction to achieve effect. Exercise and Massage are not referred to as modalities in physical therapy.

Myofascial treatment: manual therapy that concentrates on moving the fascia (connective tissue) surrounding muscle to alleviate pain.

Neurology: the study of the nervous system.

Occupational therapy: please refer to American Occupational Therapy Association (www.cota.org).

Orthopedic: pertaining to the study of bones.

Teaching hospital: hospital that is connected to a medical school and allows integration of teaching medical students and allied health students within the busy working day of the hospital.

Ultrasound: a technology that uses sound waves to deep-heat tissues. Is also used as diagnostic tool in detecting abnormalities in pregnancy.

Major Employers

U.S. Healthworks Medical Group www.ushealthworks.com
FirstHealth www.firsthealth.org
Department of Veterans Affairs www.vacareers.va.gov
Home health care at VNS www.vns.org
H Lee Moffitt Cancer Center www.moffitt.usf.edu
Memorial Sloan-Kettering Cancer Center www.mskcc.org
Cora Rehabilitation Clinics careers@corahealth.com (e-mail)

Some quality networks of acute and subacute care

Kaiser Permanente www.kaiserpermanente.org
Columbia Presbyterian www.columbiapresbyterian.com
St. Vincent's Hospital, New York City www.svcmc.org
St. Luke's Hospital, New York City www.wehealnewyork.org
Children's Hospital, Boston www.childrenshospital.org
Beth Israel, New York City www.wehealnewyork.org
University of California at San Francisco, San Francisco www.ucsfhealth.org
Alta Bates, Berkeley www.altabates.com

Helpful Web Sites

General industry sites

www.apta.org

www.apta.org/foundation

www.apta.org/bulletin

www.nlm.nih.gov/medline:us/rehabilitation

www.worldfederationinphysicaltherapy.org

www.healthyaging.org

Jobs sites

www.ptbulletin.org

www.chronicle.com (for faculty positions)

Journals/Publications

The Physical Therapy Bulletin

The Physical Therapy Journal

Cardiovascular and Pulmonary Physical Therapy: Evidence and Practice. 4th ed. Frownfelter D, Dean E. St Louis, MO 63146: Mosby Elsevier; 2006

Clinical Research in Practice: A Guide for the Bedside Scientist. Houser J, Bokovoy J. Sudbury, MA 01776: Jones and Bartlett Publishers Inc;

Exercise in Rehabilitation Medicine. 2nd ed. Frontera WR, ed. Champaign, IL 61825: Human Kinetics; 2006.

Treating Neurodevelopmental Disabilities: Clinical Research and Practice. Farmer JE, Donders J, Warschausksy, S, eds. New York, NY 10012; Guilford Publications; 2006.

Orthopedic Examination, Evaluation and Intervention: A Pocket Handbook. Dutton M. New York, NY 10121: McGraw-Hill Co Inc; 2005.

Visit Vault at **www.vault.com** for insider company profiles, expert advice, career message boards, expert resume reviews, the Vault Job Board and more.

VAULT CAREER LIBRARY   59

Accredited Physical Therapy Education Programs

Alabama
Alabama State University
The University of Alabama at Birmingham
The University of South Alabama

Arizona
AT Still University of Health Sciences
Northern Arizona University

Arkansas
Arkansas State University
University of Central Arkansas

California
Azusa Pacific University
California State University
California Sate University at Fresno, Long Beach, Northridge, Sacramento
Chapman University
Loma Linda University
Mount St. Mary's College
Samuel Merritt College
University of California, San Francisco
University of Southern California
University of the Pacific
Western University of Health Sciences

Colorado
Regis University
University of Colorado Health Sciences Center

Connecticut
Quinnipiac University
Sacred Heart University
University of Connecticut
University of Hartford

Delaware
University of Delaware

District of Columbia
The George Washington University
Howard University

Florida
Florida Agricultural and Mechanical University
Florida Gulf Coast University
Florida International University
Nova Southeastern University
University of Central Florida
University of Florida
University of Miami
University of North Florida
University of South Florida
University of St. Augustine for Health Sciences

Georgia
Armstrong Atlantic State University
Emory University
Georgia State University
Medical College of Georgia
North Georgia College and State University

Idaho
Idaho State University

Illinois
Bradley University
Governors State University
Midwestern University
Northern Illinois University
Northwestern University
Rosalind Franklin University of Medicine and Science

Indiana
Indiana University
University of Evansville
University of Indianapolis

Iowa
Clarke College
Des Moines University
St. Ambrose University
The University of Iowa

Visit Vault at www.vault.com for insider company profiles, expert advice,
career message boards, expert resume reviews, the Vault Job Board and more.

VAULT CAREER LIBRARY

61

Kansas
University of Kansas Medical Center
Wichita State University

Kentucky
Bellarmine University
University of Kentucky

Louisiana
Louisiana State University Health Sciences Center in New Orleans
Louisiana Sate University Health Sciences Center in Shreveport

Maine
Husson College
University of New England

Maryland
University of Maryland-Baltimore
University of Maryland-Eastern Shore

Massachusetts
American International College
Boston University
MGH Institute of Health Professions
Northeastern University
Simmons College
Springfield College
University of Massachusetts Lowell

Michigan
Andrews University
Central Michigan University
Grand Valley State University
Oakland University
University of Michigan-Flint
Wayne State University

Minnesota
College of St. Catherine
College of St. Scholastica
Mayo School of Health Sciences
University of Minnesota

Mississippi
University of Mississippi Medical Center

Missouri
Maryville University of Saint Louis
Missouri State University
Rockhurst University
Saint Louis University
Southwest Baptist University
University of Missouri-Columbia
Washington University of St. Louis

Montana
The University of Montana-Missoula

Nebraska
Creighton University
University of Nebraska Medical Center

Nevada
University of Nevada

New Hampshire
Franklin Pierce College

New Jersey
The Richard Stockton College of New Jersey
Rutgers, The State University of New Jersey, Graduate School at Camden
Seton Hall University
University of Medicine and Dentistry of New Jersey

New Mexico
University of New Mexico

New York
Clarkson University
College of Staten Island/The Graduate Center (CUNY)
Columbia University
Daemen College
Dominican College
D'Youville College
Hunter College
Ithaca College
Long Island University-Brooklyn Campus

Visit Vault at **www.vault.com** for insider company profiles, expert advice,
career message boards, expert resume reviews, the Vault Job Board and more.

VAULT CAREER LIBRARY   63

Mercy College
Nazareth College of Rochester
New York Institute of Technology
New York Medical College
New York University
Sage Colleges
State University of New York Downstate Medical Center
State University of New York Upstate Medical University
Stony Brook University
Touro College
University of Buffalo, State University of New York
Utica College

North Carolina
Duke University
East Carolina University
Elon University
The University of North Carolina at Chapel Hill
Western Carolina University
Winston-Salem State University

North Dakota
University of Mary
University of North Dakota

Ohio
Andrews University/Dayton
Cleveland State University
College of Mount St. Joseph
Medical College of Ohio in Consortium With Bowling Green State University and The University of Toledo
The Ohio State University
Ohio University
The University of Findlay
University of Cincinnati
Walsh University
Youngstown State University

Oklahoma
Langston University
University of Oklahoma Health Sciences Center

Oregon
Pacific University

Pennsylvania
Arcadia University
Chatham College
College Misericordia
Drexel University
Duquesne University
Gannon University
Neumann College
Saint Francis University
Slippery Rock University of Pennsylvania
Temple University
Thomas Jefferson University
University of Pittsburgh
University of Scranton
University of the Sciences in Philadelphia
Widener University

Puerto Rico
University of Puerto Rico-Medical Sciences

Rhode Island
University of Rhode Island

South Carolina
Medical University of South Carolina
University of South Carolina-Columbia

South Dakota
University of South Dakota

Tennessee
Belmont University
East Tennessee State University
Tennessee State University
The University of Tennessee at Chattanooga
The University of Tennessee Health Science Center

Texas
Angelo State University
Hardin-Simmons University
Texas State University-San Marcos
Texas Tech University Health Sciences Center
Texas Woman's University
University of Texas at El Paso
The University of Texas Health Science

Visit Vault at **www.vault.com** for insider company profiles, expert advice,
career message boards, expert resume reviews, the Vault Job Board and more.

V∧ULT CAREER LIBRARY   65

Center at San Antonio
The University of Texas Medical Branch at Galveston
University of Texas Southwestern Medical Center at Dallas
US Army-Baylor University

Utah
University of Utah

Vermont
University of Vermont

Virginia
Hampton University
Marymount University
Old Dominion University
Shenandoah University
Virginia Commonwealth University

Washington
Eastern Washington University
University of Puget Sound
University of Washington

West Virginia
West Virginia University
Wheeling Jesuit University

Wisconsin
Carroll College
Concordia University of Wisconsin
Marquette University
University of Wisconsin-La Crosse
University of Wisconsin-Madison

Canada
University of Toronto
University of Western Ontario

About the Author

Dr. Annlee Burch received her master's in physical therapy from Columbia University in 1989. She later received a master's in public health and EdD from Columbia, followed by a postdoctoral fellowship in health disparities at Columbia. Currently Dr. Burch is the director and associate professor of physical therapy at the University of Puerto Rico/Medical Sciences Campus. She has been on the faculty at Long Island University, University of New England and Mercy College. Dr. Burch lives in Santurce, Puerto Rico, with her husband, three children and dog.

Visit Vault at **www.vault.com** for insider company profiles, expert advice, career message boards, expert resume reviews, the Vault Job Board and more.

VAULT CAREER LIBRARY   67

Use the Internet's
MOST TARGETED
job search tools.

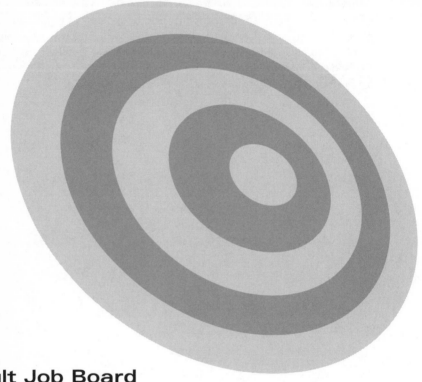

Vault Job Board

Target your search by industry, function and experience level,
and find the job openings that you want.

VaultMatch Resume Database

Vault takes matchmaking to the next level: post your resume
and customize your search by industry, function, experience
and more. We'll match job listings with your interests and
criteria and e-mail them directly to your inbox.

VAULT
> the most trusted name in career information™

GO FOR THE GOLD!